OUR
CHANGING
EARTH

EARTH'S LAYERS

Jason D. Nemeth

PowerKiDS press.

New York

Published in 2012 by The Rosen Publishing Group, Inc.
29 East 21st Street, New York, NY 10010

First Edition

Editor: Amelie von Zumbusch
Book Design: Greg Tucker

Photo Credits: Cover, pp. 4, 5, 6, 7, 8–9, 11 (top, bottom), 12, 14, 18, 19, 21, 22 Shutterstock.com; p. 10 Mike Harrington/Getty Images; p. 13 D'Arco Editori/Getty Images; p. 15 iStockphoto/Thinkstock; pp. 16–17 © Ronald Naar/age fotostock; p. 20 Nigel Treblin/AFP/Getty Images.

Library of Congress Cataloging-in-Publication Data

Nemeth, Jason D.
 Earth's layers / by Jason D. Nemeth. — 1st ed.
    p. cm. — (Our changing earth)
 Includes index.
 ISBN 978-1-4488-6169-9 (library binding) — ISBN 978-1-4488-6296-2 (pbk.) — ISBN 978-1-4488-6297-9 (6-pack)
 1. Earth—Core—Juvenile literature. 2. Earth—Crust—Juvenile literature. I. Title.
 QE509.2.N45 2012
 551.1—dc23
                              2011023998

Manufactured in the United States of America

CPSIA Compliance Information: Batch #WW12PK: For Further Information contact Rosen Publishing, New York, New York at 1-800-237-9932

CONTENTS

What do planet Earth and a hard-boiled egg have in common? They both have three layers. Like an egg, Earth has a hard outer shell called the **crust**. This is the part of Earth on which we live. Under the crust is a layer of hot rock called the **mantle**. The mantle is like the white of a boiled egg. There is an upper mantle and lower mantle.

Crust

Upper Mantle

Lower Mantle

Outer Core

Inner Core

EARTH'S LAYERS

The yolk is at the center of an egg. At the center of Earth is a layer called the **core**. The core is split into two parts. The outer core is made of liquid metal. The inner core is solid metal.

EARTH'S CENTER

The inner core of Earth is a solid ball of metal. It is about as big as the Moon and as hot as the surface of the Sun. It is made mostly of iron. Scientists think it might also have other **elements**, such as the metal nickel, in it. Elements are the basic kinds of stuff from which all things are made.

Scientists think that Earth's inner core is around 11,000° F (6,093° C). The surface of the Sun is about that hot, too. The Sun's own core is even hotter!

Earth's inner core is not the only place that iron can be found. In the crust, iron can be found mixed with other elements in rocks like this one.

The inner core is solid because of the high **pressure** at Earth's core. The pressure is the force of all of Earth's weight pressing down. Even though it is very hot, the high pressure keeps the iron from melting.

Earth's outer core is about 1,400 miles (2,253 km) thick. This makes it almost twice as thick as the inner core.

Like the inner core, the outer core is made mostly of iron with some other elements mixed in, too. The main difference between the two parts of the core is that the outer core is liquid instead of solid.

The temperature of the outer core is not known for certain. It is too far down for scientists to measure. They think that it is most likely hotter than 7,000° F (3,871° C).

The iron and other metals in Earth's outer core are liquid, just like the metal seen here.

Compasses are tools that people use to figure out which direction is north. Compasses depend on Earth's magnetic field to work.

The outer core helps create Earth's **magnetic field**. This is the area in which the pull of Earth's magnetism can be felt. Earth's magnetic field acts like a shield. It helps keep the planet safe. It keeps away harmful **particles**, or tiny things, from space.

The outer core helps keep Earth's magnetic field going. As Earth spins, the liquid iron in its outer core moves around. As the

EARTH'S MAGNETIC FIELD

liquid iron passes through Earth's current magnetic field, electricity is created. This electricity feeds into Earth's magnetic field and keeps it going strong.

Earth's magnetic field is the reason that auroras happen. These are colorful lights that can be seen in the sky in places that are far north or far south.

Like Earth's core, the mantle has two layers. They are called the upper mantle and the lower mantle. Both layers are made mostly of rock. Rock is lighter than metal. This is why the mantle floats above the core. The lower mantle is a little heavier than the upper mantle because it has some iron in it.

Some of the rock in the mantle is melted, like the rock here. Much of the rock there is solid or almost solid, though.

The upper and lower mantles combined are about 1,800 miles (2,897 km) thick. Both are made of rock that flows very slowly, like thick mud. The rock of the mantle moves because of the weight of the rock above it pressing down on it.

There is a lot of movement inside Earth. This drawing shows the currents in the outer core and the mantle.

Earth's crust is where we live. It is the hard, rocky shell that surrounds the mantle. The crust holds the oceans and the **continents**, or landmasses.

In some places, the crust is thin. Under the ocean, it may be only 5 miles (8 km) thick. Under the continents, the crust is much thicker. There it can be 25 miles (40 km) deep or more.

Giant's Causeway, along the coast of Northern Ireland, is made of the rock basalt. Basalt is the most common kind of rock in the part of the crust that lies under Earth's oceans.

Granite is the most common rock in the part of the crust that has land on it. These granite rocks are in the Seychelles, a group of islands that lie off the west coast of Africa.

The crust is broken up into about 15 pieces, called **plates**. The plates are huge slabs of rock. All of Earth's land and oceans sit on them. For example, most of the United States sits on the North American plate.

MOVING EARTH

Plate tectonics is the **scientific theory** that explains how Earth's plates fit together. Scientific theories are ideas that explain why things happen the way they do in nature.

As you know, Earth's mantle moves very slowly. Since the plates of Earth's crust float on the mantle, they move, too. Plate tectonics describes what happens where the plates bump into each other.

At times, two continents crash together. This can make mountains form. Other times, one plate goes underneath a second plate and melts back into the mantle. Sometimes two plates rub past each other. This can cause earthquakes.

Masherbrum, also known as K1, is part of the Karakorum Range. The crashing of the Indian plate into the Eurasian plate formed these mountains.

ROCK ERUPTS

Many of Earth's **volcanoes** are found where two plates meet. When one plate melts under another plate, **magma** is created. Magma is melted rock. When part of a plate melts, some of the magma sinks into the mantle. However, some magma also may rise back up to the surface. There, the melted rock spills out of volcanoes.

Melted rock is called magma when it is inside Earth. After it spills out of a volcano, the melted rock is called lava.

Sometimes magma from the mantle rises in the middle of a plate. This often happens under the ocean, where the crust is thinnest. For example, the Hawaiian Islands were formed by magma that rose up into the Pacific Ocean. When the melted rock cooled off, it formed the islands.

Here lava flows into the sea along the coast of Hawaii. When this lava cools and hardens, it will make the island a little bit bigger.

This scientist is looking at the seismic waves from an earthquake. The waves were recorded with a tool called a seismograph.

Scientists can dig and drill to study Earth's crust. The other layers are too deep to reach. Scientists must find other ways to study them. One way is to measure **seismic waves**. Seismic waves are the shakings caused by earthquakes. They travel across Earth's surface and down through its layers.

Different kinds of seismic waves travel at different speeds. The waves travel faster or slower depending on whether they are moving through solids or liquids. They move at different speeds when passing through rocks or metal. By measuring the waves' speed, scientists can tell what Earth is made of. They can also map how thick Earth's layers are.

Scientists also study Earth's crust by looking at rocks on the surface.

Earth was once a large ball of hot magma. As Earth cooled, its layers formed. The heat that remains inside Earth today supplies the energy that moves the plates and creates its magnetic field.

Earth will keep cooling, though. As it does, this energy will lessen. Plates will stop moving. The magnetic field will disappear. One day, Earth will become a big, cold rock, instead of the warm, changing planet we live on today.

Earth's core is cooling very slowly. It will be billions of years before it grows cold.

GLOSSARY

continents (KON-tuh-nents) Earth's large landmasses.

core (KOR) The hot center of Earth.

crust (KRUST) The outside of a planet.

elements (EH-luh-ments) The basic things of which all other things are made.

magma (MAG-muh) Hot, melted rock inside Earth.

magnetic field (mag-NEH-tik FEELD) A strong force made by currents that flow through metals and other matter.

mantle (MAN-tel) The middle layer of Earth.

particles (PAR-tih-kulz) Small pieces of matter.

plates (PLAYTS) The moving pieces of Earth's crust, the top layer of Earth.

plate tectonics (PLAYT tek-TAH-niks) The study of the moving pieces of Earth's crust.

pressure (PREH-shur) A force that pushes on something.

scientific theory (sy-en-TIH-fik THEE-uh-ree) An idea or group of ideas that tries to explain something in the natural world.

seismic waves (SYZ-mik WAYVZ) Waves caused by Earth's shaking.

volcanoes (vol-KAY-nohz) Openings that sometimes shoot up hot, melted rock called lava.

INDEX

WEB SITES

Due to the changing nature of Internet links, PowerKids Press has developed an online list of Web sites related to the subject of this book. This site is updated regularly. Please use this link to access the list:
www.powerkidslinks.com/chng/earth/